W9-BAI-175

Iguanodon

Written by Rupert Oliver
Illustrated by Bernard Long

Library of Congress Cataloging in Publication Data

Oliver, Rupert.
Iguanodon.

Summary: Iguanodon falls behind his herd as he searches for food, and has some life-threatening experiences.
1. Iguanodon—Juuvenile literature. [1. Iguanodon.
2. Dinosaurs] I. Long, Bernard, ill. II. Title.
QE862.065045 1984 567.9'7 84-17867
ISBN 0-86592-207-1

Rourke Enterprises, Inc.
Vero Beach, FL 32964

Rhamphorhynchus
Pteranodon
Pterodactyl
Ankylosaurus
Dimetrodon
Iguanodon
Tricondon

Iguanodon

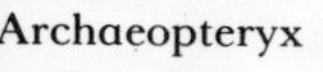
Archaeopteryx
Plesiosaurus
Ichthyosaurus
Deinonychus
Nothosaurus

Iguanodon stared into the sky and sniffed the air. He could smell rain, but it was not raining here. Far away in the mountains there was a storm. Rain was falling heavily there. That was what Iguanodon could smell.

The herd to which Iguanodon belonged had left the great forest and was moving out on to the plains. On the plains grew many delicious plants for the herd to eat. Iguanodon moved off down the slope to join his herd. He did not want to be left on his own. In the herd he would be safer from attack by a fierce Megalosaurus. This dreaded meat eater was always ready to make a meal out of an Iguanodon.

As the herd moved out on to the flat plains they kept a careful watch in case of danger. All they could see was a group of huge Cetiosauriscus. These large dinosaurs were feeding on a clump of trees in the distance.

Iguanodon went down on all fours to eat some leaves from a cycad plant. He reached out with his tongue and took a firm hold on some foliage. Iguanodon used his horny beak to nip off the leaves. Then he chewed the food with his flat teeth.

As Iguanodon pushed further into the clump of cycads there was a strange rustling sound. Suddenly three small two-legged dinosaurs emerged. They were Hypsilophodons. The Hypsilophodons looked at Iguanodon and then ran off toward the forest. They ran very quickly, bounding from one leg to the other. Iguanodon watched them for a while. Then he continued eating the juicy cycads. High above him Pterosaurs flapped and swooped through the air.

The large, rolling plain stretched as far as Iguanodon could see. It was like a vast green carpet of cycads, horsetails and rushes. Iguanodon looked hungrily at a group of maidenhair trees and monkey-puzzle trees a short distance off. They would be much tastier than the redwoods in the forest. The herd moved toward the clump of trees.

When Iguanodon looked back toward the mountains, he could see that it was still raining. However, the plains were quite dry. The rivers were almost empty. The Goniopholis had to stay in small pools of water to keep cool in the mid-day sun. The Goniopholis took no notice of the Iguanodon herd as they crossed the dry river bed.

After stopping to browse on a particularly tempting patch of horsetails, the herd reached the clump of trees. Iguanodon stretched up into the trees to reach the leaves. Using his tongue to grasp the leaves, Iguanodon munched away.

For several hours the herd stayed in the trees, then some of the Iguanodons wandered away to eat the cycads, ferns and horsetails. Others stayed at the edge of the trees and ate the leaves. Iguanodon moved deeper into the trees. He was looking for the juicy magnolia shrub which often grew under the trees. Then, Iguanodon saw some strange shapes moving in the shadows of the trees. He looked closer and suddenly gave a cry of fright and alarm.

Hiding in the trees were four Megalosaurs. These ferocious dinosaurs had powerful claws and teeth and they were hungry. Iguanodon smashed his way through the undergrowth, bellowing a warning to the rest of the herd. Behind him he could hear the thumping of the heavy feet of the Megalosaurs. As Iguanodon burst from the trees the rest of his herd scattered in alarm. Iguanodon ran on in a panic. The fierce hunters were gaining on him. He knew what would happen to him if they caught him. His life was at stake.

Iguanodon was running as fast as he could, but the Megalosaurs were overtaking him. Iguanodon's powerful legs carried him to the banks of the dried-up river. He slid down the bank to the river bed. The hungry meat eaters followed Iguanodon even here. As Iguanodon and the Megalosaurs raced along the dry river bed the Goniopholis scattered in alarm. Iguanodon looked behind him. The Megalosaurs had almost caught him. Then, he heard a strange and terrible rumbling sound.

Looking ahead of him Iguanodon could see a wall of water rushing toward him. The heavy rain in the mountains had filled the mountain streams with millions of gallons of water. That water had formed a flash flood that was pouring down the dry river bed.

When the Megalosaurs saw the rush of water they tried to run away. They were too late. The terrific force of the rushing water hit Iguanodon seconds later. It swept him off his feet and tumbled him over and over. Then, it smashed into the Megalosaurs and swept them along as well.

Iguanodon felt himself being thrown around by the water. He was being spun around by the force of the flood. Finally Iguanodon's head rose above the surface. Iguanodon took a gulp of air. He looked around and saw the Megalosaurs were also being thrown about by the water. The rushing torrent pulled Iguanodon back under the surface.

Nearby, Iguanodon could see a Polacanthus browsing on some ferns. The Polacanthus turned to look at Iguanodon. Then he went back to his meal. In the distance Iguanodon saw a herd of Iguanodons. He decided to join them.

Wearily, Iguanodon stood up on his aching legs. He set off across the plain. He passed the Polacanthus but soon had to stop to rest. Iguanodon was very tired after his adventures. After a while he went on toward the other Iguanodons.

When he was close to them he realized that they were members of his own herd. Iguanodon joined the herd. He was glad to be back with his own kind. Iguanodon fed on a clump of cycads. Soon it would be evening and the herd would settle down for the night.

Iguanodon and Early Cretaceous Europe

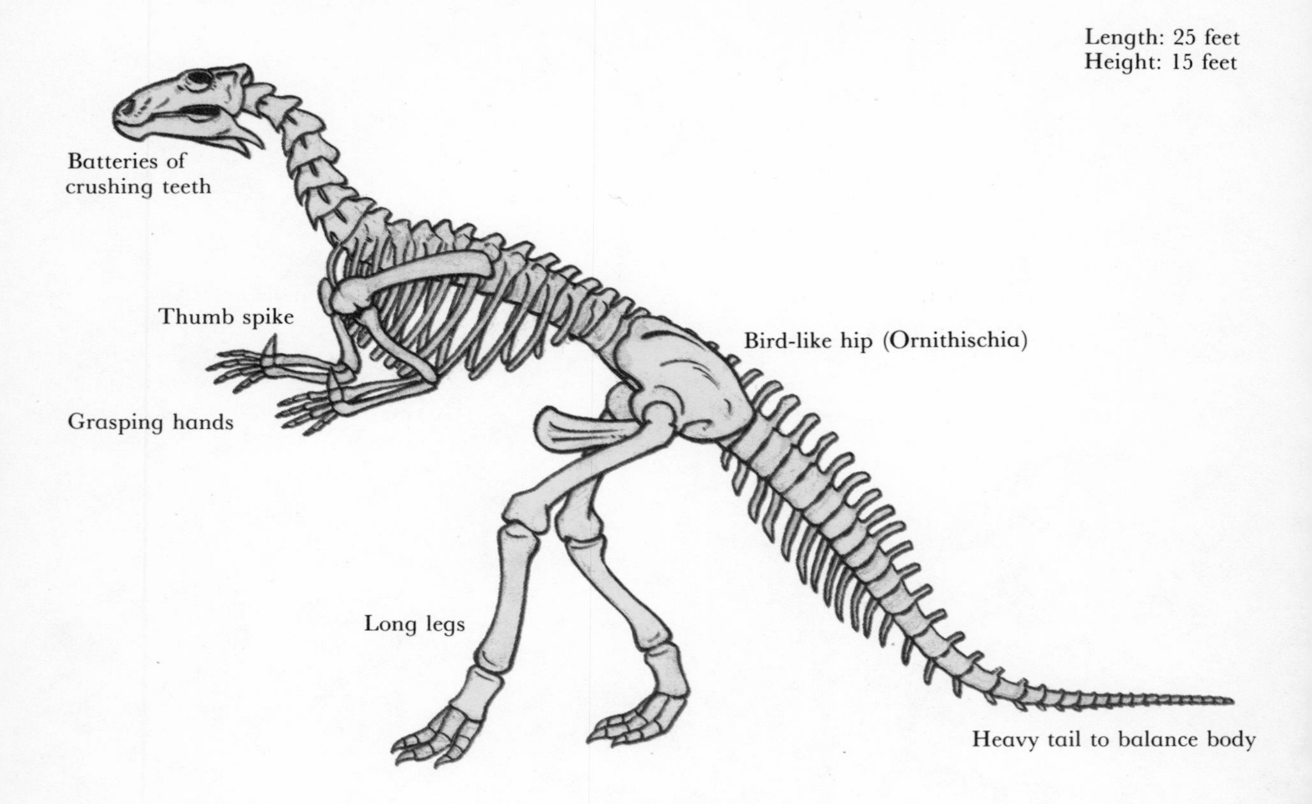

Skeleton of Iguanodon

"Iguana tooth"

Dinosaurs, like the Iguanodon, lived many millions of years ago. We only know about them today because their bones have been found in ancient rocks. But 150 years ago nobody knew about dinosaurs because their fossils had not been recognized as those of ancient reptiles.

Then, in 1822, a woman found a fossilized tooth in Sussex, England. She showed it to her husband, who was interested in fossil bones. His name was Dr. Mantell. Dr. Mantell had never seen a tooth like it, so he showed it to his scientist friends, but they did not recognize it either. Then one scientist realized that it looked like a tooth from a reptile called an iguana. Dr. Mantell called the prehistoric animal, to which the tooth had belonged, an Iguanodon, which means "iguana tooth".

It was not until many other Iguanodon bones had been found that scientists realized it was a dinosaur. One of the most important finds of Iguanodon fossils was at Maidstone, a town in England. That is why the coat of arms of Maidstone has an Iguanodon in it.

When did Iguanodon live?

Iguanodon lived 130 million years ago at the beginning of the Cretaceous period. This was the last of the periods of the Age of Dinosaurs. The first period was called the Triassic and the middle period was called the Jurassic.

Where did Iguanodon live?

Dr. Mantell found his Iguanodon tooth in Southern England. Other fossils have been found in Belgium and other places in Northern Europe. But when Iguanodon was alive, Europe was very different from today. Stretching across England where London is today, was a range of tall mountains. These are the mountains that you can see on pages 4 and 5. Below the mountains were hills covered in thick forests of conifers and cycads. To the south of the mountains and the forests was a vast lake that covered hundreds of square miles.

In those days the English Channel did not exist and the lake stretched from England right across to Europe. Iguanodon spent most of its time by this lake.

What did Iguanodon eat?

Iguanodon was a large plant-eating dinosaur of the bird-hipped group of dinosaurs. When it stood upright on its hind legs, Iguanodon was about fifteen feet high. This means that it must have been able to reach up into trees and eat the leaves, as you can see on pages 10 and 11. However, the front legs of Iguanodon were quite strong and had small hooves on them. Because of this scientists think that Iguanodon spent much of its time on all four legs browsing on small ferns and cycads.

Iguanodon had no teeth in the front of its mouth, but horny, cutting jaws. It is thought that Iguanodon had a muscular tongue and large cheeks. It would have used its tongue to grasp leaves and foliage, before nipping them off. Iguanodon would then have used its cheeks to move the food across its teeth in the back of the mouth so that it could be properly chewed. These two features would have ensured that Iguanodon was very efficient at eating plants.

Other plant-eaters

The first part of the Cretaceous period, when Iguanodon lived, was very important for the evolution of plant eating dinosaurs. The bird-hipped, or ornithischia dinosaurs were poised to take over from the lizard-hipped plant-eaters. Throughout the Jurassic period, the lizard-hipped sauropods, such as Brontosaurus, were the most common plant-eating dinosaurs. During the Cretaceous period the ornithischia, like Iguanodon, evolved into many species and became very common. For some reason this only happened in the northern parts of the world. In the south, the sauropods continued to be very common.

The Cetiosauriscus that you can see on page 6 were a type of sauropod that managed to survive in Northern Europe during the Cretaceous.

The diversity of the bird-hipped group of dinosaurs is shown by Hypsilophodon, Polacanthus and Ouranosaurus. Hypsilophodon was a small dinosaur that could run very fast. It ate the leaves and fruits of short plants and could run away from most meat-eaters. Polacanthus was a large, heavy dinosaur that could not move very fast at all. Instead, it used its impressive array of spikes and bony plates to protect itself. Ouranosaurus had a strange crest running down its back, but was otherwise very like Iguanodon. All these dinosaurs were members of the bird-hipped group, so it is not surprising that they managed to take over from the lizard-hipped group of dinosaurs as the most important plant-eaters.

Ouranosaurus, an African relative of Iguanodon which had a 'sail' along its back.